Meg Elisabeth is a poet and writer from South-East England. She is currently a Liberal Arts student at the University of Nottingham and hopes to be writing full-time once she has graduated. Meg spends most of her free time either reading (mostly fantasy) or writing her own poems and novels. She intends to publish her first novel as soon as she can and is beyond excited for more of her work to reach the world. As a 22-year-old, Meg takes great pride in her achievements so far and encourages each and every young person with a passion for writing to never stop chasing their dreams.

To anyone struggling with their mental health, I hope you can
see yourself in these pages and be reminded that
You are not alone.

Meg Elisabeth

MEMOIRS OF AN ANXIOUS PERSON

AUSTIN MACAULEY PUBLISHERS™

LONDON • CAMBRIDGE • NEW YORK • SHARJAH

ISBN 9781398488427 (Paperback)
ISBN 9781398488434 (ePub e-book)

www.austinmacauley.com

First Published 2024
Austin Macauley Publishers Ltd®
1 Canada Square
Canary Wharf
London
E14 5AA

Thank you to my family, near and far, who believed in me and always encouraged my passion to write.

To my friends, for your overly-dramatic squeals and gasps and sobs when I read you my poems. You brought them to life.

To my colleagues who helped me find the happiness and strength I needed to start to overcome my anxiety. You are the turning point of this anthology.

To my publishers, without whom I would never have been able to share my journey with the world. I am forever grateful.

Downhill

I didn't cry when we arrived
Or when you left me
Or when I found myself surrounded by strangers

I was happy for two weeks
I felt comfortable and safe
But something must have happened
Because time changed pace

My mind tripped downhill
My thread unravelled
The bubble around me closed in
Its pop was the sound of my helpless cry

Suddenly I was hungry,
I was tired and lonely and scared
The strangers were my friends,
But I only wanted you

Three more weeks went by
And the hill was still rolling

So I gave in and let myself cry
I sobbed and I panicked as I kept falling down

You found me eventually
Bruised at the bottom of the hill
You picked me up gently, and away we went
The vast world before us

But there's still time to pass,
Before I dare re-climb the hill

The Kitchen

I tremble by my door
Darkness seems to swallow me
Fight or flight?
I fly

I will not tread beyond the threshold
One step will take me from Paradise into Edom

Hours and days and weeks merge together
Hunger burning at their centre
But still, I will not tread beyond
Until the threshold takes me home

Sometimes We Lose

Today I was beaten
Bested by my mind and its knife-sharp thoughts
Trounced by the cruel voice that keeps me from myself

But I still feel like a winner
A conqueror
I know my own needs
And best always comes from bad

Sometimes we lose
But losing shouldn't feel like an end
When it could be a blessed beginning

Job Interview

My eyes stare but do not see
My fingers clench but the pain is distant
All I feel is the pounding of my heart
The tension that arcs through me
As I try in vain to control my breathing

My face is red and tear-stained
But my eyes are dry
I feel the car rock beneath my feet
The movement steadies me
But at the thought of my destination
Tears threaten to be dragged from my eyes once more

The car stops, and I take a shaky breath
Without thinking, I open my door and step outside
The door thuds closed behind me
But my feet refuse to move
I cannot go anywhere at all

Tears trickle down my cheeks like rain
And in that moment, I hate myself
But the anger doesn't pierce the adamant wall of fear
I am left alone with a stranger,
And the tears are still falling

Nauseous

It jumps and batters against its cage
It races and sprints but never tires
It booms and rings; a warning bell

It heaves and tightens as it fights
It convulses and flutters relentlessly
It drowns, battling against the darkness

It churns and rolls in pain and fear
It screams and shouts but cannot be saved
It pleads in desperation

It stops

Dreams on Stages

I am floating on silken clouds
A swan-white dress pools around me
My hair lifts in a breeze that is not there

Somewhere in the near distance
I feel my mouth open,
Preparing to sing for him
I watch eagerly from afar
But no sound emerges

My throat squeezes
My box bursts
But he cannot see me struggle
His tight lips are unforgiving

He watches soundlessly
Waiting for me to cross the fine line

Somewhere far away
I feel my heart pound
I feel my breath quicken
And my hands turn slick
I desperately want to please him
He mustn't be disappointed, he mustn't hate me

In one gasp, the stage is gone
And so is he
But my heart still pounds
And it is no longer distant

The Driver's Seat

I'm in a new place
With traffic and lights and horns

People yell, people swear
There is only noise

But in truth, it is perfectly quiet
And the driver's seat is comfortable beneath me

The road is long and leisurely winding
No cars are in sight

But the traffic and lights and horns are still there
So the driver's seat must stay empty

Just Me and the Dog

The road is narrow and busy
The pavement stretches for miles
And the only thing between us is a lead
A long, red line

It keeps her safe

She pulls and tugs playfully
Trying to find new smells and friends
But my grip only tightens
My heart hurts
But I won't let go

It keeps her safe

Just Before I Go to Sleep

Every night is the same
Just before I go to sleep
A monster comes to find me
He makes me feel unsafe

Every night is the same
Just before I go to sleep
My bed becomes a prison
I am a slave to my mind

Every night is the same
Just before I go to sleep
My skin crawls until I am someone else
I won't find me again until morning

Every night is the same
Just before I go to sleep
Shivers keep me rudely awake
They are relentless in my consciousness

Let me sleep
So the monster leaves me be

Looking Back

Once you see it, it's everywhere
In your past
Your present
Your future

You find it beside you
Because it's always been there
A part of you
Unnoticed for too long

But now that you recognise its teeth
You see the countless marks it's left
Its bites cover your body
And they cannot be healed

If you can't find its beginning
How could you possibly reach its end?

My New Therapist

He's kind
With a warm smile
And a soothing accent
When he talks
It's easy to listen

But he's still a stranger
And when I speak
I don't recognise what I'm saying
I don't tell him what I feel
I can't explain

By the second session
It's a little easier
But now, maybe *he* doesn't know
Doesn't quite understand
He still listens
Even though I've convinced myself,
He cannot help me

The Park in Lindfield

People
Everywhere, people

Squabbling children
Playing football
Walking dogs
Pushing prams
Crying babies
Riding bicycles

People
Everywhere, people

Tomorrow Never Comes

They say "Tomorrow never comes"
So why is it all I can think of?
And why can I never understand it?

They say "Tomorrow never comes"
So why must I obsess over it?
And why do they tell me it matters?

They say "Tomorrow never comes"
So why can't I get it off my mind?

New Environment

Sometimes it's not as scary as you think
Sometimes it's better
Sometimes it's easier

Don't run to your darkness,
Just because it's familiar
Don't hide from the light

New Environment 1.1

A fur-lined blanket on a winter's night
A bubble that floats with me inside
The sound of laughter that I brought to life
The smile of a sister as she holds you tight

The easy conversation of two lifelong friends
The welcome breeze on a scorching summer's day
A hand always reaching when the light starts to fade
A supporting grip that evokes steady sanity

New Environment 1.2

Sometimes sweet is bitter
But not with you
Your sweet is easy to swallow

Your sweet is kind
Comforting and thoughtful
A relief, a welcoming

The sweet of a mother
Of a wise older sister
Of an aunt or grandmother

A sweet that never tires
It stays, unrelentingly calm
It keeps me steady

New Environment 1.3

How does fragile become strong?
How is silence replaced with ceaseless chatter?
How do colleagues turn into friends?
How can you treasure something so brief?

How can you miss someone before you've even left?

New Environment 1.4

A mirror must sit in the corridor
Surely you're an illusion
An older, sweeter, blonder version of me
A friend on the other side of the hall

Oh, how I'd hope your illusion would be there each day
Waiting to share a laugh between stories

Soon, your world will be far away
And the mirror will be gone from the hall
But I will always remember Mrs Jackson
And the gentle way we reflected

New Environment 1.5

I push my money through the slot,
And I choose a song,
Hoping to dance just once
But the Jukebox is broken
And bouncing music pours out
Ruthlessly incessant

My feet tire of dancing quickly
But the music will not let me stop,
Until all your songs have been sung
Soon, the ache becomes oddly familiar
So each and every dreary night
I return to the broken Jukebox

I love dancing to your music
All your melodies are my favourite

New Environment 1.6

Easy talk, easy silence
Easy smile, easy laughter
Easy questions, easy answers

Hard goodbyes

New Environment 1.7

My new was your new too
Your uncertainty
I felt it as though it were mine

It was sweet to grow together
To gradually familiarise
To find home in a new environment

Metamorphosis

For months I was the rabbit
The terrified, helpless prey

Then I changed, I strengthened
Until I became the coy fox

But now I am the wolf
Silver and brave and proud

Now I am me, truly me
An alpha, a warrior

A survivor

The Train to Bournemouth (Relapse)

Twenty minutes early
It calms me
Soothes me
But not quite enough

I still feel the nausea burning in my throat,
But I push it down
Push it back inside
Try my best to take a breath

It's all in my head
It isn't even real
I'll be okay,
Won't I?

I feel hyper
Uncomfortably alert
Watching out for everything and everyone

Am I safe?
Am I on the right train?
Will I be on time?
Will my ticket work?

Questions
Useless, unnecessary questions
They won't go away
They circle my mind like vultures

But I learn to let them pass
Let them crash over me like a wave
I acknowledge them,
And then force them to flow past
Unanswered
I'll feel better soon

BXY

Unfamiliar and new and wildly exciting
Butterflies fluttered inside me
But Phobos could not claim me today
I did not fear, I *craved*

So, I explored with you
And you secured something in that fearing part of me
The incorporeal personification of "practice makes perfect"

And though I am far from perfect,
(At least in your respect)
Practising with you feels simpler than before

The Driver's Seat is no longer empty

So Society Says

So Society says…
"Smile and sing, then you'll be happy
Sadness is nothing but a chore
Solitude is simply curable"

So Society says…
"Socialise and speak a thousand words
Silence shouldn't be pleasure
Shame isn't so easily shared"

So Society says…
"Some people live but everybody fights
Surely the fight should be fair
Sickness has no place in war"

Society has no place in peace

Poetry Can't Do Everything

Poetry is the best descriptor
Poetry is the strongest communicator
But even poetry can't tell this story

The story of two rights
Who lived through a time of wrong
The story of friends becoming strangers

The End felt so close
Its cruel talons ready to strike
But we pushed it back
Refused its bleak image

Instead, as strangers we met again
And as friends once more, we parted
Two rights no longer held in wrong time

Maybe poetry can't do everything
But ours can

Tell the Truth

The grass isn't deep enough to drown me
The sun isn't hot enough to scorch
Your gaze isn't sad enough to quiet me
There is no excuse
No reason not to simply tell the truth

Things I've hidden are suddenly let free
Words I shy from daily, gladly leave through parted lips
Feelings and thoughts and tempestuous doubts,
They've finally found a way out
Now I live with the knowledge that I told the truth

Shivers take minutes and hours to pass
Shakes and nausea grip me firmly by the hand
No supper or chatter or warmth can draw them away
But I could never regret it
Never be ashamed of telling you the truth

Round Two

Panic fills my lungs,
Quashing out the air
My eyes are sliced open
Tears fall freely

I can't stay
I can't live here
I just want to go home
The panic is unbearable

Please don't leave me here

I Think I'll be Okay

The first evening was easy
The first night was hard

The first morning was strange
The first afternoon was exciting

The second evening was surprising
The second night was easier

The third morning was welcoming
It was kind

It won't be easy
I'll have to be brave

But time will make me stronger
I think I'll be okay

An Introvert in A Crowd

The howl of a lone wolf is melancholy
An omega lost in a world of sorrow
But there is a beauty in its solitary note
A call that must be answered

The howl of a pack is harmonious
An alpha leading its betas through a world of joy
But there is sadness in its full sound
A call that is drowned out by many

The pack is welcoming and trusting
But the lone wolf still needs time to be alone
Her howl is free

My Eyes Always Find Yours

Honey-brown flecked with amber
Mesmerising
I let them drown me
I am your willing victim

No words have been spoken alone
No time has been spent between us
But still, my eyes always find yours
And they are toxic in their beauty

It hurts to be near you
And the pain is bitter
But your nectar is excruciatingly sweet
If I lose myself, at least I'll be lost in you

And maybe one day your eyes will find mine too

The Art of Being Calm

Hours and hours pass in your company
With lips never closed
And ears always open
Somehow, you've found me
And taught me the art of being calm

Thank you
Thank you for teaching me
I will pray each day to keep you
And to never find myself without you
You've been burned onto my heart

Found Freedom

It exists in some fantasy world
Where magic reigns free,
And dragons dance in the sky
It finds home among mountains and seas

Perhaps in a dank dungeon,
Where terror and pain are slick in the air
Or beneath the crystalline ocean,
Among merpeople who fight for peace

It is the stuff of war
Of sword against shield, magic against human
Maybe it is found where animals talk
And it settles down in vast forests or dingy cities

Through trauma and mistrust
Between rivals and friends
It squeezes its way into their words
Into the unsuspecting minds

That's where I found it
But not where it found me